THE
QUOTABLE
CAT

THE

QUOTABLE CAT

A CAT LOVER'S COMPENDIUM OF OBSERVATIONS ON THE FELICITOUS FELINE

LISA A. ROGAK

CONTEMPORARY BOOKS

A TRIBUNE NEW MEDIA/EDUCATION COMPANY

Library of Congress Cataloging-in-Publication Data

Rogak, Lisa Angowski.
    The quotable cat : a cat lover's compendium of observations on the
felicitous feline / Lisa Angowski Rogak.
      p.   cm.
    ISBN 0-8092-3941-8 (cloth)
    1. Cats—Quotations, maxims, etc.   I. Title.
PN6084.C23R6   1992
808.8'2—dc20

                                        92-273
                                        CIP

Acknowledgments can be found at the end of the book.

Published by Contemporary Books, Inc.
Two Prudential Plaza, Chicago, Illinois 60601-6790
Manufactured in the United States of America
Library of Congress Catalog Card Number: 88-17700
International Standard Book Number: 0-8092-3941-8

TO MARGO, SQUGGY, AND PINKY

Contents

THE ESSENTIAL CAT

I cannot exist without a cat. . . . Life would not be
worth living without a cat.

PEGGY BACON

Cats are forever.

FRANCOIS FOSSIER

A harmless necessary cat.

WILLIAM SHAKESPEARE

There is something about the presence of a cat . . .
that seems to take the bite out of being alone.

LOUIS J. CAMUTI

CATS AND CURS

The affections of the dog . . . may be held firm by fear; but Pussy, if you behave too ignobly towards her, will cease to love you. . . . She will not allow herself to love where she has ceased to respect.

ROSAMUND BALL MARRIOTT WATSON

For a dog to chase, frighten, annoy, and worry a cat is to do the cat a mischief.

CONNECTICUT SUPREME COURT RULING, 1901

Wouldn't You like someday
to put a curse on the whole race of dogs?
If so, I should say, Amen.

BERNOS DE GASZTOLD

There is a natural antipathy between the cat and the dog. The very presence of a cat in the wake of a dog is a challenge, an insult, a bait, and an enticement. Fido will run after Thomas.

JUDGE HIGGINS, RULING IN A TENNESSEE COURTROOM, 1914

The Dog gives himself the Airs of a Cat.

RICHARD STEELE

To respect a cat is the beginning of the aesthetic sense. At a stage of culture when utility governs all of its judgments, mankind prefers the dog.

UNKNOWN

The visionary chooses a cat; the man of concrete a dog. Hamlet must have kept a cat. Platonists, or cat lovers, include sailors, painters, poets, and pickpockets. Aristotelians, or dog lovers, include soldiers, football players, and burglars.

UNKNOWN

Even the stupidest cat seems to know more than any dog.

ELEANOR CLARK

A cat will sit washing his face within two inches of a dog in the most frantic state of barking rage, if the dog be chained.

CARL VAN VECHTEN

The dog for the man, the cat for the woman.

ENGLISH PROVERB

If animals could speak . . . , the dog would be a
blunt, outspoken, honest fellow, but the cat would
have the rare talent of never saying a word too much.

PHILIP GILBERT HAMERTON

THE CAT AND THE CANARY

She: The cat has eaten our pet bird;
He: The wicked beast shall die.
Then he resumed his quail on toast
And she ate pigeon pie.

UNKNOWN

Whenever I sing, he comes and sniffs my song all
around my mouth; he tries to find it with his claws,
to make off with it.

MARCEL JOUHANDEAU, ON HIS
CAT'S REACTIONS TO HIS BIRD CALLS

Cats are required to wear three bells to warn birds
of their approach.

LAW IN LEMONINE, MONTANA

They call me cruel. Do I know if mouse or song-bird feels
I only know they make me light and salutary meals.

C. S. CALVERLEY

If cats had wings there would be no ducks in the lake.

INDIAN PROVERB

Cats are forbidden from chasing a duck down a city street.

LAW IN MORRISBURG, LOUISIANA

Pity the little cats, who did not commit the Original Sin and who did not eat birds in Paradise, where all Animals lived in peace.

MARCEL UZE

CATS AND CATS

Friendship between cats can exist, but more or less in the same way that it can exist for a not very sociable man who spends his time in provoking others, and who, when asked why he does not have any friends, replies: "I would like to have them . . . but they are so ignoble!"

FRENCH PSYCHOLOGIST PAUL LEYHAUSEN,
COMPARING CATS WITH PARANOID HUMANS

Dynasties of cats, as numerous as the dynasties of the Pharaohs, succeeded each other under my roof. . . . The memory of the cats we have lost fades like the memory of men.

THEOPHILE GAUTIER

There wanst was two cats in Kilkenny,
Aitch thought there was one cat too many;
So they quarrelled and fit,
They scratched and they bit,
Till, excepting their nails,
And the tips of their tails,
Instead of two cats, there wasn't any.

KATHERINE ELEANOR CONWAY

Ah! little do you know how swiftly fly
The venomed darts of feline jealousy.

ROBERT SOUTHEY

If a cat is creeping up on prey and realizes that
another cat is watching, it will straighten up and act
disinterested.

PAUL LEYHAUSEN

Quite obviously a cat trusts human beings; but she doesn't trust a cat because she knows her better than we do.

KAREL CAPEK

Two cats can live as cheaply as one, and their owner has twice as much fun.

LLOYD ALEXANDER

Although the cats have long lived together under the same roof, all is not sweetness and light. They take fiendish delight in scaring and chasing each other. The tormentor and the pursued change regularly. These disagreements do not seem serious, but more on the order of cheap thrills.

DAVID LOVE

CAT PEOPLE

The cat lives his own life; he expects you to live yours.

NELSON A. CRAWFORD

The catlike man is one upon whom no tricks can be played with success.

DELPHINE GAY

Free to a good home—female cat or husband. Husband says either he goes or cat goes. Cat fixed, husband isn't.

WANT AD IN FLINT, MICHIGAN,
WEEKLY WORLD NEWS

You will always be lucky if you know how to make friends with strange cats.

AMERICAN COLONIAL PROVERB

If a cat scratches you, you will be disappointed that day.

AMERICAN COLONIAL PROVERB

Few people are mugwumps about the cat.

WILLIAM H. A. CARR

There is one way in which cats differ from all other animals and that is in the effect they have on human beings.

PATRICIA DALE-GREEN

I have myself found, the result of many years enquiry and study, that all people who keep cats . . . do not suffer from those petty ailments which all flesh is heir to.

LOUIS WAIN

Cat people are different, to the extent that they generally are not conformists. How could they be, with a cat running their lives?

LOUIS J. CAMUTI

Cats are like greatness: Some people are born into cat-loving families, some achieve cats, and some have cats thrust upon them.

WILLIAM H. A. CARR

Maybe in the future we should add one more question to those we ask of presidential candidates. In addition to asking where they stand on Rhodesian chrome and socialized medicine, we should ask them where they stand on cats.

Better still, we should demand to see the cats these candidates say they have raised, just to make sure we are not having the fur pulled over our eyes.

MARYLAND CONGRESSMAN GILBERT GUDE,
IN A 1976 SPEECH

STUBBORN CATS

Cats don't like change without their consent.

ROGER A. CARAS

Essentially, you do not so much teach your cat as bribe him.

LYNN HOLLYN

Don't use cats—they'll screw up your data.

UNKNOWN SCIENCE PROFESSOR TO STUDENT

If a cat can detect no self-advantage in what it is being told to do, it says the hell with it, and, if pressure is brought to bear, it will grow increasingly surly and irritable to the point where it is hopeless to continue.

JOHN D. MACDONALD

15

CAT CHOW

[A Gentleman Cat approaches food] slowly . . . ,
however hungry he may be, . . . and decides at least
three feet away what his verdict is going to be: Good,
Fair, Passable or Unworthy. . . . if it is Unworthy, he
will perform the rite of pretending to scratch earth
over it and bury it.

MAY SARTON

[It] ate beefsteak and cockroaches, caterpillars and
fish, chicken and butterflies, mosquito hawks and
roast mutton, hash and tumblebugs, beetles and pigs'
feet, crabs and spiders, moths and poached eggs,
oysters and earthworms, ham and mice, rats and rice
pudding, until its belly became a realization of Noah's
Ark.

LAFCADIO HEARN

A plate is distasteful to a cat, a newspaper still worse; they like to eat sticky pieces of meat sitting on a cushioned chair or a nice Persian rug.

MARGARET BENSON

If left to their own devices, felines tend to nap and nibble throughout the day and night, scarcely differentiating between the two.

LYNN HOLLYN

Take a cat, nourish it well with milk
And tender meat, make it a couch of silk,
But let it see a mouse along the wall
And it abandons milk and meat and all.

GEOFFREY CHAUCER

Never will you get a better psychological subject than a hungry cat.

DR. EDWARD LEE THORNDIKE

When cat people get together they are as single-minded as vegetarians, or kelp and soybean addicts. For they can talk for hours about what their cats will and will not eat. Once you meet a cat lover you will pursue his or her cat's food predilections endlessly.

GLADYS TABOR

The cat that has its mouth burned by drinking hot milk will not drink even buttermilk without first blowing upon it.

INDIAN PROVERB

There once was a cat named Knishes,
Who ate lots of fattening dishes.
When put on a diet,
He caused such a riot—
His owner, he meowed, was delicious.

SUZANNE WEAVER

They are to be served daily, in a clean and proper
manner, with two meals of meat-soup, the same as we
eat ourselves, but it is to be given them separately in
two soup-plates. The bread is not to be cut up into
the soup, but must be broken into squares about the
size of a nut, otherwise they will refuse to eat it. A
ration of meat, finely minced, is to be added to it; the
whole is then to be mildly seasoned, put into a clean
pan, covered close, and carefully simmered before it
is dished up.

LAST WILL AND TESTAMENT OF
17TH-CENTURY FRENCH HARPIST MADAME DUPUIS,
PROVIDING FOR THE CARE OF HER TWO CATS.

THE FEMININE FELINE

Froward women were made from cats, just as most virtuous, industrious matrons were developed from beer.

UNKNOWN

I would have in my house—a reasonable woman—a cat moving among the books.

UNKNOWN

If a girl treads on a cat's tail, she will not find a husband before a year is out.

FRENCH PROVERB

The greedy cat makes the servant girl watchful.

FRENCH PROVERB

Of all the creatures in this world, cats an' women has the hardest time.

UNKNOWN

I think of a woman as something like myself.

PAUL GALLICO, TRANSLATING FROM CAT LANGUAGE

I have found my love of cats most helpful in understanding women.

JOHN SIMON

An overdressed woman is like a cat dressed in saffron.

EGYPTIAN PROVERB

THE CAT IN THE MIRROR

Which is the more beautiful, feline movement or feline stillness?

ELIZABETH HAMILTON

If to her share some feline errors fall,
Look in her face, and you'll forgive them all.

UNKNOWN

Handsome cats and fat dungheaps are the sign of a good farmer.

FRENCH PROVERB

If one owns a pretty cat, it's best to avoid the furrier.

JACOB CATS

Here lies a pretty cat:
its mistress, who never loved anyone,
loved it madly;
Why bother to say so? Everyone can see it.

EPITAPH ON TOMBSTONE OF CAT WITH
FULL-RELIEF DETAIL OF THE DECEASED

The love of dress is very marked in this attractive
animal. He is proud of the lustre of his coat, and
cannot endure that a hair of it shall lie the wrong
way.

JULES CHAMPFLEURY

A cat must either have beauty and breeding, or it
must have a profession.

MARGARET BENSON

NINE LIVES

She knows that nine lives are enough.

OSWALD BARRON

Cats have nine lives, onions and women seven skins.

PROVERB

Tho' Two and Two make four by rule of line,
Or they make Twenty-two by Logic fine,
Of all the figures one may fathom, I
Shall ne'er be floored by anything but Nine.

OLIVER HERFORD

"John Harvard" was famous, not only because, in spite of her name, she produced three kittens, but because on the night when the family decided to get rid of her, she warned them, by her mewing, of a conflagration, and thus saved not only their four lives, but her own nine.

GEORGINA STICKLAND GATES

A cat has nine lives and a woman has nine cats' lives.

ENGLISH PROVERB

If you take even one of a cat's nine lives, it will haunt you forever.

UNKNOWN

THE CAT AND THE PEN

He had a habit of coming to my study in the morning, sitting quietly by my side or on the table for hours, watching the pen run over the paper, occasionally swinging his tail round for a blotter, and then going to sleep among the papers by the inkstand. Or, more rarely, he would watch the writing from a perch on my shoulder. Writing always interested him, and, until he understood it, he wanted to hold the pen.

CHARLES DUDLEY WARNER

A catless writer is almost inconceivable. It's a perverse taste, really, since it would be easier to write with a herd of buffalo in the room than even one cat; they make nests in the notes and bite the end of the pen and walk on the typewriter keys.

BARBARA HOLLAND

If it be true that all remarkable human beings resemble animals, then Walt Whitman was like a cat—a great old grey Angora Tom, alert in response, serenely blinking under his combed waves of hair, with eyes inscrutably dreaming.

EDMUND GOSSE

Outside of a cat, a book is man's best friend. Inside of a cat, it's too dark to read.

ROBERT ERICSON,
LILAC HEDGE BOOKSHOP, NORWICH, VERMONT

Cats like silence, order, and quietness, and no place is so proper for them as the study of a man of letters.

UNKNOWN

The affinity of writers for cats is something that has never been satisfactorily explained.

WILLIAM H. A. CARR

It is impossible for a writer to stay ahead of a cat.

VICKI HEARNE

A Poet's Cat, sedate and grave
As poet well could wish to have,
Was much addicted to inquire
For nooks to which she might retire,
And where, secure as mouse in chink,
She might repose, or sit and think.

WILLIAM COWPER

THE FREELANCE FELINE

You may own a cat, but cannot govern one.

KATE SANBORN

I value in the cat the independent and almost ungrateful temper which prevents it from attaching itself to anyone, the indifference with which it passes from the salon to the housetop.

The cat lives alone, has no need of society, does not obey except when it likes, pretends to sleep that it may see the more clearly, and scratches everything that it can scratch.

FRANCOIS CHATEAUBRIAND

It is always diverting to find something . . . but to find a cat: that is unheard of! For you must agree with me that . . . even though it belongs to us now, it remains somehow apart, outside, and thus we always have:

$$\text{life} + \text{a cat}$$

Which, I can assure you, adds up to an incalculable sum.

RAINER MARIA RILKE

There is no animal that loves freedom as does this one.

CESARE RIPA

Everyone knows that cats are *always* the bosses, no matter where they may find themselves.

RUTHVEN TODD

Cats are the only really free creatures on earth.

ANN CHADWICK

How lucky to be a cat
Free to accept or—refuse
What is offered!

UNKNOWN

No cat ain't damn fool enough to let itself be trained
to do extra work.

UNKNOWN BROADWAY STAGEHAND

The only domestic animal man has never conquered.

UNKNOWN

31

Cats easily assume the habits of society, but never acquire its manners.

COUNT DE BUFFON

It is in the nature of cats to do a certain amount of unescorted roaming.

ADLAI STEVENSON

Work—other people's work—is an intolerable idea to a cat. Can you picture cats herding sheep or agreeing to pull a cart? They will not inconvenience themselves to the slightest degree.

LOUIS J. CAMUTI

It is useless to punish a cat. They have no conception of human discipline; if they do, the idea is unattractive to them.

LLOYD ALEXANDER

He will be your friend if he deems you worthy of friendship, but not your slave. . . . Yet what confidence is implicit in his steadfast companionship.

THEOPHILE GAUTIER

THE SIXTH SENSE

The cats know when a bomb's about to fall.
How do they know such things? They know, that's
    all

UNKNOWN

A cat will desert a ship about to start on its last
voyage, and there is evidence to show that sailors
have refused to undertake voyages following the
desertion of the ship's cat.

SUPERSTITION

If your cat is left-pawed, he's probably one hell of a
psychic.

UNKNOWN

THE CAT HOUSE

Passion for place—there is no greater urge in feline nature.

PAUL ANNIXTER

Cats attach themselves to places rather than persons and are rather harbored than owned. They are not subject to direction like dogs, nor can they be put under the same restraint as other domestic animals.

PENNSYLVANIA COURT DECISION

The cat tribe possesses lairs to which they return.

GEORGINA STICKLAND GATES

It is less to the walls of the house that [the cat] clings than to a certain arrangement of objects, of furniture, which bear more than the house itself the trace of personality.

MADAME MICHELET

To keep a cat home, butter its feet.

PROVERB

The cat has its own compass that works through the electrical strength of its fur being attracted by either the negative or positive poles of the earth, thus pointing it in one direction or another.

LOUIS WAIN

Even a cat is a lion in her own lair.

INDIAN PROVERB

If a neighbor's cat wanders around your home, it means the neighbors are gossiping about you.

PROVERB

When those who do not know cats find themselves in a house which is given over to them, they generally want to have the thing explained.

PAMELA KELLINO AND JAMES MASON

Books and cats and fair-haired little girls make the best furnishing for a room.

FRENCH PROVERB

People are forbidden from entering a darkened house which does not have a cat living in it.

TALMUD

If cats desert a house, illness will always reign there.

UNKNOWN

Black cats keep care and trouble away from the house. It is lucky for a black and strange cat to stray into anybody's house.

WELSH FOLKTALE

A good-looking Persian cat is an ornamental piece of furniture in a house.

G. H. POWELL

38

CAT CALLS

Good liquor will make a cat speak.

UNKNOWN

You who do not realize the value of music,
Come along and hear the magnificent concert,
The enchanting tunes I teach my cats.
Since my beautiful voice makes even these animals
     amenable,
I cannot fail to instruct you all.

17TH-CENTURY POSTER FOR CONCERT
WITH MEOWING AND PURRING CATS

The cat sings a brave treble in her own language.

THOMAS MIDDLETON

If you speak cat at all there is no reason why you should not speak it fluently. It is simply a matter of application.

SYLVIA TOWNSEND WARNER

If we treated everyone we meet with the same affection we bestow upon our favorite cat, they, too, would purr.

MARTIN BUXBAUM

Rubbing himself against my cheek he purred like the kettle-drums in Berlioz's *Requiem*.

CARL VAN VECHTEN

With Cats, some say, one rule is true:
Don't speak till you are spoken to.

T. S. ELIOT

Cats use their voices much as a means of expression,
and they utter under various emotions and desires at
least six or seven different sounds. The purr of
satisfaction which is made during both inspiration and
expiration, is one of the most curious.

CHARLES DARWIN

Her purrs and mews so evenly kept time,
She purred in metre and she mewed in rhyme.

JOSEPH GREEN

41

She whurleth with her voice, having as many tunes
as turnes, for she hath one voice to beg and complain,
another to testifie her delight and pleasure, another
among her own kind . . . in so much as some have
thought that [cats] have a peculiar intelligible
language among themselves.

EDWARD TOPSELL

His voice is tenderly discreet;
    But let it be serene or vexed
Still always it is sonorous and profound,
    This is his charm and his secret.

BAUDELAIRE

We cats are all capable of talking, had we not
acquired from human beings a contempt for speech.

LUDWIG TIECK

Cats, as anyone who has ever been awakened by one knows, are very vocal suitors, whose "sweet nothings" range from low-pitched cries to contented purrs of requited love.

LYNN HOLLYN

No animal on earth is as capable of expressing itself as the cat.

WILLIAM H. A. CARR

To please himself only a cat purrs.

UNKNOWN

Providence wisely has not allowed the cat to speak any language but his own.

UNKNOWN

Even if you have just destroyed a Ming vase, purr.
Usually all will be forgiven.

LENNY RUBENSTEIN

Cats seem to go on the principle that it never does
any harm to ask for what you want.

JOSEPH WOOD KRUTCH

Cats never squeal on each other.

LOUIS J. CAMUTI

THE LEGAL CAT

The animals whose tail, eyes, and life are of equal worth: a calf, a filly from common work, and a cat, excepting the cat that shall watch the King's barn.

WELSH LEGAL CODES, CIRCA A.D. 940

Most judges are cat lovers.

CARL VAN VECHTEN

Senators and representatives . . . go very slowly in formulating laws regarding the cat. They know perfectly well that the cat will refuse to obey these laws.

CARL VAN VECHTEN

The cat gave the man a list of rules which he copied on a slip of paper. The rules were:

Do Not Kick Cats
No Atomic Wars
No Mousetraps
Kill the Dogs

"If the world does not obey these rules, we will simply eliminate the race," said the cat, and then closed his eyes and yawned and stretched and promptly went to sleep.

SPENCER HOLST

The husband took the cat if there was but one; if there were others they went to the wife.

OLD WELSH DIVORCE CODE

Rest assured that your cat will not respect any man-made laws.

H. J. DEUTSCH, D.V.M.

The common law says that a cat is entitled to one bite. After that, it's the owner's fault.

UNKNOWN

Any cat that runs in the street after dusk is required to wear a headlight.

DALLAS, TEXAS, LAW

People are forbidden from going barefoot in a house where a cat dwells.

TALMUD

The cat is not of a species of animals naturally inclined to mischief, such as, for example, cattle, whose instinct is to rove and whose practice is to eat and trample down growing crops.

CONNECTICUT SUPREME COURT DECISION
(EARLY TWENTIETH CENTURY)

CATS AND FISH

Pure herring oil [is] the Port Wine of English Cats.

HONORE DE BALZAC

The cat loves fish, but does not like to wet her paws.

ENGLISH PROVERB

What female heart can gold despise?
What cat's averse to fish?

THOMAS GRAY

When human folk at table eat
A kitten must not mew for meat,
Or jump to grab it from the dish
(Unless it happens to be fish).

49

OLIVER HERFORD

THE CAT AS MOUSER

The Mouse should stand in Feare,
    So should the squeaking Rat;
All this would I do if I were
    Converted to a Cat.

GEORGE TURBERVILLE

Well-fed cats are the best mousers.

NELSON A. CRAWFORD

The borrowed cat catches no mice.

JAPANESE PROVERB

A bashful cat makes a proud mouse.

PROVERB

Cats do not keep the mice away; . . . they preserve them for the chase.

OSWALD BARRON

Wherever the mice laugh at the cat, there you will find a hole.

PORTUGUESE PROVERB

What is that which never was and never will be? A mouse's nest in a cat's ear.

KATE SANBORN

When cat and mouse agree, the farmer has no chance.

DANISH PROVERB

A mouse in the paws is worth two in the pantry.

LOUIS WAIN

He who hunts with cats will catch only rats.

JACOB CATS

A lame cat is better than a swift horse when rats infest the palace.

CHINESE PROVERB

Thou victim of my paw
By well-established law.

AESOP

He that denies the cat skimmed milk must give the
mouse cream.

PROVERB

People who hate cats were rats in another
incarnation.

PROVERB

It is better to feed one cat than many mice.

NORWEGIAN PROVERB

Love to eat them mousies
Mousies what I love to eat
Bite they little heads off
Nibble on they tiny feet.

B. KLIBAN

ON THE INFERIORITY OF HUMANS

If men and women would become more feline,
indeed, I think it would prove the salvation of the
human race.

CARL VAN VECHTEN

Surely such cats are better than such men.

COSMO MONKHOUSE

I fear that a salute in front of a cat is in bad taste. In
the eyes of any cat we human beings are all of
equal—and, I suspect, quite low—rank.

NELSON A. CRAWFORD

I have studied many philosophers and several cats.
The wisdom of the cats is vastly superior.

HIPPOLYTE TAINE

In nearly all lovers of cats one finds a certain
contempt for the stupidity of mankind.

NELSON A. CRAWFORD

To err is human
To purr feline.

ROBERT BYRNE

Who can tell what just criticisms the cat may be
passing on us beings of wider speculation?

GEORGE ELIOT

Would any sane cat actually *choose* to become human?

CLAIRE NECKER

Cats look down upon us, dogs look up to us, pigs is equal.

UNKNOWN

I can say with sincerity that I like cats. A cat is an animal which has more human feelings than almost any other.

EMILY BRONTE

This morning I hate my better nature. I much prefer my cat.

GERALD BULLETT

To understand the character of a cat, to respect her independence, to recognize and deplore her pitiless instincts, to be charmed by her gentler moods, to admire her beauty, to appreciate her intelligence, and to love her steadfastly without being loved in return—these things are not often possible to the Anglo-Saxon nature.

AGNES REPPLIER

It seems that when man has considered himself to be the master of all things, the cat has been shunned and feared, being the visible evidence that man could not control everything. On the other hand, when man acknowledged the power of unknown and mysterious forces, then the cat was respected and accepted as an equal.

H. L. COOKE

To a cat, we are probably not much more than a big obstacle much of the time. Cats don't bump into us unless they want a good bit of rubbing or they want to stake a claim on our ankles or our dining-room chair.

ROGER A. CARAS

Before a Cat will condescend
To treat you as a trusted friend,
Some little token of esteem
Is needed, like a dish of cream.

T. S. ELIOT

Man is a kind of locomotive tree, pleasant to rub against, the lower limbs of which afford a comfortable seat, and from whose upper branches occasionally drop tidbits of mutton and other luscious fruit.

UNKNOWN

Any cat passing out of the front door after dark was
to be regarded as His Excellency, the Governor, and
to be saluted accordingly.

GENERAL SIR THOMAS EDWARD GORDON

It is perhaps easier for a cat to train a man than for a
man to train a cat. A cat who desires to live with
human beings makes it his business to see that the so-
called superior race behaves in the proper manner
toward him.

CARL VAN VECHTEN

A cat has absolute emotional honesty: human beings,
for one reason or another, may hide their feelings,
but a cat does not.

ERNEST HEMINGWAY

People must be very puzzling to cats, since cats are above most animals rational and direct. Cats whisper to one another about people, courteously pretending that they are merely washing one another's ears.

FRANCES AND RICHARD LOCKRIDGE

What sort of philosophers are we who know absolutely nothing of the origin and destiny of cats?

HENRY DAVID THOREAU

A cat's got her own opinion of human beings. She don't say much, but you can tell enough to make you anxious not to hear the whole of it.

JEROME K. JEROME

FELINE FROLICS

Cats are like Baptists. They raise hell but you can't catch them at it.

UNKNOWN

Care once killed a cat.

PROVERB

A cat's heart is normally excited.

COLETTE

To pounce well, your cat must pounce often.

LYNN HOLLYN

When she plays, she doesn't seem to say: Man, I'm glad that I've got you here. She can play by a deathbed. With her paw she will toy with a corner of the shroud.

KAREL CAPEK

When you see your person settle down to do some fireside or after-dinner reading, jump up into his or her lap, get comfortable, and then put your paws across the book or paper. This will make turning the pages difficult, and after a while you will find they will give up.

PAUL GALLICO

CAT'S CRADLE

People with spare kittens to give are as persuasive as
a real estate agent with a cut-over swamp on his
hands.

MARGARET COOPER GAY

Peace is a Persian cat basking on your best brocaded
cushion—two or three kittens staggering and
tumbling around and over her.

PAUL ANNIXTER

A house is never perfectly furnished for enjoyment
unless there is a child in it rising three years old, and
a kitten rising three weeks.

ROBERT SOUTHEY

The cat in youth is a full lecherous beast.

BARTOLOMEUS ANGLICUS

Gather kittens while you may,
  Time brings only sorrow;
And the kittens of today
  Will be old cats tomorrow.

OLIVER HERFORD

A cat with little ones has never a good mouthful.

FRENCH PROVERB

A kitten is the delight of a household. All day long a
comedy is played by this incomparable actor.

JULES CHAMPFLEURY

65

I sometimes think the Pussy-Willows grey
Are Angel Kittens who have lost their way.

OLIVER HERFORD

May is kitten month. We are knee-deep.

SPOKESPERSON FOR THE ASPCA, NEW YORK CITY

An ordinary kitten will ask more questions than any
five-year-old boy.

CARL VAN VECHTEN

The joys of motherhood are not part of your pet's
goals in life.

ZERO PET POPULATION GROWTH

Nothing is more charming than such a cat's maternal happiness; you ought to have a cat for yourself, if for nothing else but for those kittens.

KAREL CAPEK

Even cat haters often like kittens.

WILLIAM H. A. CARR

Nothing's more playful than a young cat, nor more grave than an old one.

THOMAS FULLER

I wish I had a litter of kittens scampering over the typewriter right now—there's no better excuse to stop working.

MARGARET COOPER GAY

Kittens can happen to anyone.

PAUL GALLICO

Like mothers everywhere, the cat has her work cut
out for her. She must train her offspring in almost all
phases of activity. This is fortunate, because cats
simply refuse to learn from humans.

ERIC GURNEY

Cats mean kittens, plentiful and frequent.

DORIS LESSING

I call my kittens Shall and Will because no one can
tell them apart.

CHRISTOPHER MORLEY

No matter how much cats fight, there always seem to be plenty of kittens.

ABRAHAM LINCOLN

The cause of the maternal intemperance of English cats, who threaten to populate the whole world, has not yet been decided.

HONORE DE BALZAC

THE FAMILY TREE

Cats, more than any other creatures, have held out against time and change. Pearl never emulated the human, wished only to be what she was and had always been, and cleaved to the grim old days when she was the biggest and fiercest, with claws like Druid war-sickles and saber fangs, curved and hollowed for the sucking of blood. Nature had dwarfed her kind for the good of other tribes, but rarely was she conscious of the fact.

PAUL ANNIXTER

Cat mistakes are the kind of "accidental" errors, biological "setbacks" chargeable to civilization and to domestication. They have nothing in common with clumsy, blunt actions that are almost intentional.

COLETTE

Noah thereupon passed his hand down the back of the lion. The king of the beasts sneezed and a cat leapt out of its nose.

ANGELO S. RAPPOPORT

The cat is not really a domestic animal, and his chief charm lies in the fact that he still walks by himself.

KONRAD LORENZ

How could we think of reproaching roses with this marvelous system of defense which we so dread in cats?

JULES CHAMPFLEURY

CAT NOMENCLATURE

Cats must have three names—an everyday name,
such as Peter; a more particular, dignified name, such
as Quaxo, Bombalurina, or Jellylorum; and, thirdly,
the name the cat thinks up for himself, his deep and
inscrutable singular Name.

T. S. ELIOT

We tie bright ribbons around their necks, and
occasionally little tinkling bells, and we affect to
think that they are as sweet and vapid as the coy
name "kitty" by which we call them would imply. It
is a curious illusion.

ALAN DEVOE

They say the test of this is whether a man can write an inscription. I say, "Can he name a kitten?" And by this test I am condemned, for I cannot.

SAMUEL BUTLER

[My cats] died early—on account of being so overweighted with their names, it was thought— "Sour Mash," "Apollinaris," "Zoroaster," "Blatherskite," . . . names given them, not in an unfriendly spirit, but merely to practice the children in large and difficult styles of pronunciation. It was a very happy idea—I mean, for the children.

MARK TWAIN

Do our cats name us? My former husband swore that
Humphrey and Dolly and Bean Blossom called me
The Big Hamburger.

ELEANORA WALKER

Our cat had been called various names, but none of
them stuck. Melissa and Franny; Marilyn and Sappho;
Circe and Ayesha and Suzette. But in conversation, in
love talk, she miaowed and purred and throated in
response to the long-drawn-out syllables of
adjectives—beee*oooo*ti-ful, de*lic*ious puss.

DORIS LESSING

It is difficult to explain why anyone would take the
trouble to give a good home to a cat, to love and care
for it, and then to give it a disparaging name.

JACOB ANTELYES, D.V.M.

74

If given time, a cat will name itself. We have prematurely named a newcomer, only to have it correct us later. For example, Mouse began life as Fat Minnie. Eventually, she slimmed down and took to bringing us mice or leftover mouse parts in the middle of the night.

DAVID LOVE

CAT LOVE

I love cats, I adore cats, and may be forgiven for
putting one in the sky, after sixty years of hard work.

FRENCH ASTRONOMER J. J. L. DE LALANDE,
ON HIS EFFORTS TO LAUNCH A CAT INTO SPACE.

Momma loves morals and Papa loves cats.

SUSY CLEMENS, MARK TWAIN'S DAUGHTER

In the matter of animals I love only cats, but I love
them unreasonably for their qualities and in spite of
their numerous faults. I have only one, but I could
not live without a cat.

J. K. HUYSMANS

Sometimes he sits at your feet looking into your face with an expression so gentle and caressing that the depth of his gaze startles you. Who can believe that there is no soul behind those luminous eyes!

THEOPHILE GAUTIER

My cat good.

KOKO, A FEMALE GORILLA SIGNING TO ZOOKEEPERS ABOUT HER MANX KITTEN, WHICH SHE NAMED LIPS-LIPSTICK.

I am indebted to the species of the cat for a particular kind of honorable deceit, for a great control over myself, for a characteristic aversion to brutal sounds, and for the need to keep silent for long periods of time.

COLETTE

Whoever cares well for cats will marry as happily as he or she could wish.

FRENCH PROVERB

The cat is not a commonplace creature when she loves.

M. FEE

Why, it is asked, should we humble ourselves to win the fluctuating affections of a cat? Why indeed, save that some of us most desire that which is difficult to obtain.

AGNES REPPLIER

The more I see of people, the more I love my cat.

BUMPER STICKER

There are few things in life more heartwarming than to be welcomed by a cat.

TAY HOHOFF

I'll tell you something interesting about cats. Everybody thinks that *their* cats are the best. They don't feel that way about anything else—they don't think their wives or their cars or even their dogs are the best—but they all think their cats are just terrific.

MICHAEL O'DONOGHUE

The cat always leaves her mark upon her friends.

SPANISH PROVERB

Dogs are disciplined, horses are enslaved, cows and pigs are exploited. Only cats join us as opportunistic partners. They do things for us, we do things for them, and when both sides feel like it we share the pleasure of each others' company.

JAN MORRIS

The cat has too much spirit to have no heart.

ERNEST MENAULT

THE AMOROUS CAT

Whenever the cat of the house is black,
The lasses of lovers will have no lack.

OLD ENGLISH COUPLET

In March lengthening days trigger hormones in cats
which lead from one thing to another and result in a
new generation of cats every May.

ATLANTIC MONTHLY, MAY 1991

If a cat washes her face in front of several persons,
the first person she looks at will be the first to get
married.

EARLY AMERICAN SAYING

How could anyone prefer, I have frequently asked myself, the bare bony form of a human, male or female, to the perfection of a feline, whether thrillingly predatory in the shape of a cheetah, or voluptuously tantalizing in that of my own preference, an Abyssinian cat?

JAN MORRIS

Every waking moment was precious to her; in it she would find something useful to do—and if she ran out of material and couldn't find anything else to do she would have kittens.

MARK TWAIN, DESCRIBING HIS CAT SOUR MASH

No workman can build a door proof against a cat or a lover.

FRENCH SAYING

One has never known cats until one has lived for the week or ten days it lasts with a female cat in search of a mate.

FRANCES AND RICHARD LOCKRIDGE

The male cat is not much as a father. He is like the happy Frenchman, a bachelor at heart.

ERIC GURNEY

THE ARTISTIC CAT

One would think a cat had painted it!

EDGAR DEGAS, ON THE QUALITY OF RENOIR'S PAINTING

It is odd that, notwithstanding the extreme beauty of cats, their elegance of motion, the variety and intensity of their colour, they should be so little painted by considerable artists.

PHILIP GILBERT HAMERTON

Painting cats is a question of genius.

THEOPHILE GAUTIER

Nothing is so difficult as to paint the cat's face,
which as Moncrif justly observes, bears a character of
"finesse and hilarity." The lines are so delicate, the
eyes so strange, the movements subject to such
sudden impulses, that one should be feline oneself to
attempt to portray such a subject.

JULES CHAMPFLEURY

PROUD PUSS

The greatest privilege of Cats is to depart with the grace that characterizes your actions, and let no one know where you are going to make your little toilets.

HONORE DE BALZAC

They are too proud for their own good.

ROGER A. CARAS

She will attempt nothing that she cannot do well.

K. C. MCINTOSH

RHYMING CATS

Zinnias and cats
are equivalent democrats.
Zinnias and cats
are a detached sufficiency
a cool liberty.

NELSON A. CRAWFORD

To whom none ever said scat,
No worthier cat
Ever sat on a mat
Or caught a rat:
Requies—cat!

JOHN GREENLEAF WHITTIER

He blinks upon the hearth-rug,
And yawns in deep content,
Accepting all the comforts
That Providence has sent.

Louder he purrs, and louder,
In one glad hymn of praise
For all the night's adventures,
For quiet, restful days.

Life will go on for ever,
With all that cat can wish:
Warmth and the glad procession
Of fish and milk and fish.

Only—the thought disturbs him—
He's noticed once or twice,
The times are somehow breeding
A nimbler race of mice.

ALEXANDER GRAY

If I lost my little cat, I should be sad without it.
I should ask St. Jerome what to do about it,
I should ask St. Jerome, just because of that
He's the only Saint I know that kept a pussy-cat.

CHILDREN'S POEM

LUNAR CATS

Though such things may appear to carry an air of
fiction with them, it may be depended on that the
pupils of her eyes seem to fill up and grow large upon
the full of the moon and to decrease again and
diminish in brightness on its waning.

PLUTARCH

Just as the lion is a creature that belongs to the sun,
so is the cat a lunatic beast—that is, a beast governed
by the moon.

VULSAN DE LA COLOMBIERE

The cat went here and there
And the moon spun round like a top,
And the nearest kin of the moon,
The creeping cat, looked up.

W. B. YEATS

The qualities of a cat are that it be perfect of ear,
perfect of eye, perfect of teeth, perfect of tail, perfect
of claw, and without marks of fire; and that it will
kill mice well; and that it shall not devour its kittens;
and that it be not caterwauling on every new moon.

OLD WELSH CODE

The cat has always been associated with the moon.
Like the moon it comes to life at night, escaping from
humanity and wandering over housetops with its eyes
beaming out through the darkness.

PATRICIA DALE-GREEN

CATS AND CHILDREN

Cats and children make wonderful companions because cats have sense enough to go climb a tree when the play becomes too boisterous.

MARGARET COOPER GAY

The child's attitude toward the cat is largely anthropomorphic. He attributes to the cat the same thoughts and feelings which he himself experiences and in his treatment of his pet unconsciously reveals his own standards of right and wrong, his tests of affection, his preferences and dislikes.

G. STANLEY HALL, M.D.

No cat has ever said, "I love you," except to the sensitive ears of children.

FRANCES AND RICHARD LOCKRIDGE

A word of caution: never, under any circumstances, retaliate with tooth or claw for anything a child might do to you. For if you are so much as suspected of having scratched their Precious, even in play, you will find yourselves back in the alley before you can say *felix domesticus*.

PAUL GALLICO

For some strange reason children's cats are all alike, all limp, all dirty, all hungry, and all gentle.

MARGARET COOPER GAY

CAT'S EYE

Cat eyes tell the time of day.

CHINESE PROVERB

When the pupil of a cat's eye broadens, there will be rain.

WELSH PROVERB

They watch you when they want to. You watch them . . . when they want you to. It is the very essence of being a cat.

ROGER A. CARAS

It is in their eyes that their magic resides.

ARTHUR SYMONS

Small cat pupils mean low tide; large pupils mean high tide.

UNKNOWN

Why do cats close their eyes when drinking milk? . . .
Because if Allah asks them whether they've had their
milk, they stand a better chance of getting more
because they can truthfully say they haven't seen any.

MOSLEM FOLK TALE

Cat's eyes are gems or marbles or the reflectors along
highways which guide motorists driving in the dark.

MURIEL BEADLE

If I stare into the face of
my fifteen-year-old cat
I do not regret the lack of journeys.
For when I look into his
contracting, dilating pupils
I travel in depth.

NEVILLE BRAYBROOKE

Cat eyes seem a bridge to a world beyond the one we know.

LYNN HOLLYN

Meeting the human eye is one of the things a cat does best and most often.

FRANCES AND RICHARD LOCKRIDGE

The male Cat doth also vary his eyes with the Sun; for when the Sun ariseth, the apple of his eye is long; toward noon it is round, and at the evening it cannot be seen at all, but the whole eye sheweth alike.

EDWARD TOPSELL

A cat is not a conscience; I'm not
saying that.
What I'm saying is

why are they looking?

JOHN L'HEUREUX

But the thing about cats is first of all that they are looking at us, and perhaps the thing about ailurophobes is that they don't want to be looked at like that.

VICKI HEARNE

CATNAPS

You all day long, beside the fire,
Retrace in dreams your dark desire,
  And mournfully complain
In grave displeasure, if I raise
Your languid form to pet or praise;
  And so to sleep again.

ARTHUR BENSON

Kittens are born with their eyes shut. They open
them in about six days, take a look around, then
close them again for the better part of their natural
lives.

STEPHEN BAKER

A little drowsing cat is an image of perfect beatitude.

JULES CHAMPFLEURY

Let sleeping cats lie.

FRENCH PROVERB

CATS AND WEATHER

If the cat washes her face o'er the ear,
'Tis a sign that weather'll be fair and clear.

WILLIAM HENDERSON

Scratch but thine ear,
Then boldly tell what weather's drawing near.

LORD WESTMORELAND

True calendars as pusses eare,
Wash't o'er to tell what change is neare.

ROBERT HERRICK

Cats coveting the fire more than ordinary or licking
their feet or trimming the hair of their heads and
mustachios presage a storm.

FRENCH SAYING

When a cat looks out a window, a storm's coming.

UNKNOWN

If a cat puts a paw above her head, company's
coming.

UNKNOWN

When a cat licks its tail, a visitor will come from the
direction its tail is pointing.

UNKNOWN

While rain depends, the pensive cat gives o'er
Her frolics, and pursues her tail no more.

JONATHAN SWIFT

If the cat's fur is shiny, the weather will be fair.

UNKNOWN

When a cat sharpens her claws, the wind will come
from the direction her tail points.

UNKNOWN

The weather will change if a cat sneezes.

UNKNOWN

THE INTELLIGENT CAT

A cat of genius is never without resources.

TABITHA GRIMALKIN

Thousands of cats on thousands of occasions sit helplessly yowling, and no one takes thought of it or writes to his friend the professor; but let one cat claw at the knob of a door, supposedly as a signal to be let out, and straightway this cat becomes representative of the cat-mind in all the books.

E. L. THORNDIKE

Intelligence in the cat is underrated.

LOUIS WAIN

A recent census taken among cats shows that approximately 100 percent are neurotic. That estimate is probably on the low side.

STEPHEN BAKER

My cat never laughs or cries; he is always reasoning.

UNAMUNO

Cats never make the same mistake twice.

UNKNOWN

In the understanding of mechanical appliances cats attain to a higher level than any other animals, except monkeys and perhaps elephants.

GEORGE J. ROMANES

Anyone who has ever known a cat really well feels
that this cat is superior to most Harvard professors in
brain power.

GLADYS TABOR

A cat bitten once by a snake dreads even rope.

ARAB PROVERB

The cat with the straw tail sitteth not near the fire.

PROVERB

The cat always uses precisely the necessary force;
other animals roughly employ what strength they
happen to possess without reference to the small
occasion.

PHILIP GILBERT HAMERTON

THE MYSTERIOUS CAT

There is no answer to most questions about the cat.
She has kept herself wrapped in mystery for some
3,000 years, and there's no use trying to solve her
now.

VIRGINIA RODERICK

Avenging cats are merely giving back in kind what
they received.

CLAIRE NECKER

The cat is cryptic, and close to strange things which
men cannot see.

H. P. LOVECRAFT

The cat remains an enigma.

DENNIS C. TURNER

In the eyes of the superstitious, there is scarcely a
movement of the cat which is not supposed to have
some significance.

T. F. THISELTON DYER

Any normal, ordinary cat can keep any human being
in a state of frustration.

GLADYS TABOR

My cats are compromised. I do not entirely trust
them—they may be spies, like dolphins, reporting to
some unknown authority.

JAN MORRIS

It is remarkable, in cats, that the outer life they reveal to their masters is one of perpetual confident boredom. All they betray of the hidden life is by means of symbol; if it were not for the recurring evidences of murder—the disemboweled rabbits, the headless flickers, the torn squirrels—we should forever imagine our cats to be simple pets whose highest ambition is to sleep in the best soft chair, whose worst crime is to sharpen their claws on the carpeting.

ROBLEY WILSON, JR.

THE ALOOF CAT

The cat gives the world nothing and receives from it everything.

GEORGINA STICKLAND GATES

As soon as they're out of your sight, you are out of their mind.

WALTER DE LA MARE

THE HEDONISTIC CAT

Cats can be very cooperative when something feels good, which, to a cat, is the way everything is supposed to feel as much of the time as possible.

ROGER A. CARAS

Not that a cat's life is unbearable, but . . . it is filled with so many temptations.

CLAIRE NECKER

CAT EUPHORIA

'Twas that reviving herb, that Spicy Weed,
The Cat-Nip. Tho' 'tis good in time of need,
Ah, feed upon it lightly, for who knows
To what unlovely antics it may lead.

OLIVER HERFORD

My cat has taken to mulled port and rum punch.
Poor old dear! He is all the better for it.

JEROME K. JEROME

Catnip is vodka and whisky to most cats.

CARL VAN VECHTEN

111

When the sun goes down, I split from home,
Take my catnip, and I get stoned!
Now that's why I get high
To forget I'm a pet.

NANCY DOLENSEK AND BILL ROGERS

Catnip will always really belong to cats. When it comes to going into ecstasies over the plant, we are not much of a match and can only watch from the sidelines, wondering what it is all about.

VICKY MCMILLAN

Cats are forbidden from drinking beer.

LAW IN NATCHEZ, MISSISSIPPI

CATS AND WATER

To bathe a cat takes brute force, perseverance,
courage of conviction—and a cat. The last ingredient
is usually the hardest to come by.

STEPHEN BAKER

Cats are popularly supposed to dislike wet, but I
have seen two of them in a steady rain conduct an
interview with all the gravity and deliberation for
which these affairs are celebrated.

OLIVE THORNE MILLER

It is bad luck to cross a stream carrying a cat in your
arms.

FRENCH PROVERB

Why people should prefer a wet cat to a dry one I have never been able to understand; but that a wet cat is practically sure of being taken in and gushed over, while a dry cat is liable to have the garden hose turned upon it, is an undoubted fact.

JEROME K. JEROME

A scalded cat dreads even cold water.

FRENCH PROVERB

A catt will never drowne if she sees the shore.

FRANCIS BACON

THE VALUABLE CAT

The worth of a kitten from the night it is kittened until it shall open its eyes is a legal penny; and from that time until it shall kill mice, two legal pence; and after it shall kill mice, four legal pence; and so it always remains.

OLD WELSH CODE

It's too dangerous a journey to risk the cat's life.

CHARLES A. LINDBERGH, EXPLAINING WHY HIS KITTEN, PATSY, WOULDN'T ACCOMPANY HIM ON HIS HISTORIC 1927 TRANSATLANTIC FLIGHT.

The cat is the only animal that is not taxed.

UNKNOWN

The old legal tradition that a cat is valuable property still survives in the United States. The courts have ruled that "A cat which is kept as a household pet may properly be considered a thing of value. It ministers to the pleasures of its owner."

BURTON TAUBER

THE STRAY CAT

To keep a stray cat from wandering, put some of its fur in your shoes.

UNKNOWN

To keep a stray cat, let it see itself in a mirror.

UNKNOWN

Bring a cat home blindfolded and throw it on the middle of a bed, and it will never leave.

UNKNOWN

CAT TAILS

Said the cat, and he was Manx,
   "Oh, Captain Noah, wait!
I'll catch the mice to give you thanks,
   And pay for being late."
So the cat got in, but oh,
His tail was a bit too slow.

OLD ENGLISH RHYME

The tail in cats is the principal organ of emotional expression.

ALDOUS HUXLEY

Cats talk with their tails.

CLEVELAND AMORY

Noah, sailing o'er the seas,
   Ran fast aground on Ararat.
His dog then made a spring and took
   The tail from off a pretty cat.
Puss through the window quick did fly,
   And bravely through the waters swam,
Nor ever stopp'd till high and dry
   She landed on the Calf of Man.

Thus tailless Puss earn'd Mona's thanks,
And ever after was call'd Manx.

ANOTHER OLD ENGLISH RHYME

CLEAN CATS

If you have committed any kind of an error and anyone scolds you—wash. If you slip and fall off something and somebody laughs at you—wash.

If somebody calls you and you don't care to come and still you don't wish to make it a direct insult—wash. Something hurt you? Wash it.

PAUL GALLICO

ACKNOWLEDGMENTS

Quotes by Stephen Baker from *How to Live with a Neurotic Cat*, copyright © 1985 by Stephen Baker; reprinted by permission of Warner Books, Inc., New York.

Quotes by Roger Caras from *A Cat Is Watching*, copyright © 1989 by Roger Caras; reprinted by permission of Simon & Schuster, Inc.

Quotes by William H. A. Carr from *The Basic Book of the Cat*, copyright © 1963 by William H. A. Carr; reprinted with permission of Charles Scribner's Sons, an imprint of Macmillan Publishing Company.

Quotes by Eric Gurney from *The Calculating Cat*, copyright © 1990, 1962 by Eric Gurney; reprinted by permission of Prentice Hall, a division of Simon & Schuster, Englewood Cliffs, N.J.

INDEX

A

Aesop, 53
Alexander, Lloyd, 10, 33
Amory, Cleveland, 118
Anglicus, Bartolemeus, 65
Annixter, Paul, 35, 64, 70
Antelyes, Jacob, D.V.M., 74

B

Bacon, Francis, 114
Bacon, Peggy, 1
Baker, Stephen, 98, 104, 113
Barron, Oswald, 24, 51
Baudelaire, 41

C

H

J

K

L

Lessing, Doris, 68, 74
Leyhausen, Paul, 8, 9
L'Heureax, John, 97
Lincoln, Abraham, 69
Lindbergh, Charles, 115
Lockridge, Frances, 61, 83, 93, 96
Lockridge, Richard, 61, 83, 93, 96
Lorenz, Konrad, 71
Love, David, 10, 75
Lovecraft, H.P., 106

M

MacDonald, John, 15
Mason, James, 37
McIntosh, K. C., 86
McMillan, Vicky, 112
Menault, Ernest, 80

R

Rainer, Maria Rilke, 30
Rappoport, Angelo S., 71
Repplier, Agnes, 58, 78
Ripa, Cesare, 30
Roderick, Virginia, 106
Rogers, Bill, 112
Romanes, George J., 104
Rubenstein, Lenny, 44

S

Sanborn, Kate, 29, 51
Sarton, May, 16
Shakespeare, William, 1
Simon, John, 21
Southey, Robert, 9, 64
Steele, Richard, 3
Stevenson, Adlai, 32

U

Unamuno, 104
Uzé, Marcel, 7

V

Van Vechten, Carl, 4, 40, 45, 55, 60, 66, 111

W

Wain, Louis, 13, 36, 52, 103
Walker, Eleanora, 74
Warner, Charles Dudley, 26
Warner, Sylvia Townsend, 40
Watson, Rosamund Ball Marriott, 2

Y